Board Fund Raising Manual

Aspen Publishers, Inc.

From the publishers of "Board Fund Raising Strategies" newsletter

Reproduction of this manual is strictly forbidden, except for designated pages. Quotations must have the consent of the publisher. This publication is designed to provide accurate and authoritative information in regard to the subject matter covered. It is sold with the understanding that the publisher is not engaged in legal, accounting or other professional services. If legal or other expert assistance is required, the services of a competent professional should be sought. (From a Declaration of Principles jointly adopted by a committee of the American Bar Association and a committee of publishers.) Laws vary from state to state, so some material may not apply to you. Aspen Publishers does not necessarily endorse any products or services mentioned. To order more copies of this manual, contact Aspen Publishers, Inc., 7201 McKinney Circle, Frederick, MD 21701 or 1-800-638-8437. Editorial offices are located at 150 Third Street, Box 226, Akron, IA 51001. Please send editorial comments to this address or phone 712/568-2418. Editor: Darla Struck.
ISBN # 0-8342-0405-3
©ASPEN PUBLISHERS, INC., 1992

Contents

Chapter 1	**How to galvanize your board into an effective fund raising body**	1
Chapter 2	**How to put together a first-rate fund raising team**	7
Chapter 3	**Use your personal connections to find donors and dollars**	15
Chapter 4	**Use your business connections to uncover money and support for your nonprofit**	23
Chapter 5	**Asking donors for money**	31
Chapter 6	**Make your special event outstanding in every way**	43
Chapter 7	**How to conduct major fund raising campaigns**	53
Chapter 8	**Planned giving is an excellent source of money for your nonprofit**	67

CHAPTER 1

How to galvanize your board into an effective fund raising body

The crisis in funding..2
Dedicated board members make the difference..............2
Board members are your Number One fund raisers.....3
The first big step: Commit yourself to fund raising!.....3
Your wildest dreams can come true!...............................4
Grab a piece of the $818 million charitable
    contribution pie!..5

Your nonprofit's expenses are up, and you're finding the dollars harder than ever to come by. It's a familiar refrain these days. It's also why effective fund raising is so important to the health of your nonprofit.

As board members, you're in an excellent position to make sure that the donations and gifts keep coming in. Your fund raising leadership is truly the key to your nonprofit's continued success.

Potential donors, who are feeling an economic pinch this year, are going to be more selective about which organizations they give to. This will test your board's fund raising ability to the max. That's why you need to know the most effective methods and strategies to bring in those charitable contributions!

The crisis in funding

We recently conducted a survey of 1,500 nonprofit administrators from all over the US and Canada to find out what concerns are uppermost in their minds. Almost to a person, administrators said they wish board members would play a more active role in fund raising!

Just listen to this frustrated administrator who sums up the situation many nonprofits face these days...

"My board and I ran head-on into a budget deficit this year," he says. "It's not the first deficit we've had, but it's certainly the largest in our nonprofit's history.

"In the past, I've been able to do my own fund raising to keep our deficits down. But lately both costs and the demand for our services keep rising--and I'm not sure how we'll be able to get rid of our current deficit.

"Up to now, my board has been hesitant to become involved in fund raising," this administrator tells me. "Board members have told me to cut spending--which I've done. But you can only cut so much before you have to eliminate programs and services. I'm concerned about the future of this organization. There's so much we could do if we had the money--I only wish I knew some way to motivate my board to go out and raise it."

Dedicated board members make the difference

Even if you and your fellow board members have never had to ask for donations, the fiscal reality of these tough times may change that. In fact, the future of your nonprofit may depend largely on your board's skill at raising charitable contributions.

Asking others for donations is an uncomfortable experience for many people. But when you consider the alternative--cutting services or even closing your doors--it's worth a little initial discomfort. Take it from someone in a position to know...

"You don't want to let funding get to the crisis stage where you have to cut back on necessities," says Board Chairwoman Connie Christenson (Grand Rapids, MI). "It's better for a nonprofit's board to be fiscally responsible and put in the fund raising time than to suffer the effects of not meeting a budget.

"I've been on other boards where board members didn't realize fund raising was a part of their job--but it simply has to be!" she says.

Board members are your Number One fund raisers

As a board member, you need to be aware of the powerful influence you have in your community. When you give a presentation to a civic group asking it to support your nonprofit, you're far more persuasive than your nonprofit's administrator or staff.

Why? For the simple reason that you're not on the payroll. When others see you represent your nonprofit as a board member, they see an unselfish volunteer lending a helping hand to people.

This plays right into your hands as a board fund raiser. It also highlights an important point about fund raising: You need to make the most of your time, **talents** and resources in going after the maximum amount of available fund raising **dollars** in your community--because you have the greatest opportunity for success!

Most boards get into fund raising because they face a financial crisis. But truly successful board members continue to raise money long after the crisis is over. Why? Because they've discovered that they have the power to make their organization grow and prosper!

They've accomplished this by thinking **BIG**. Pancake breakfasts and car washes are fine, but they're small events that bring in small amounts of money. A talented and aggressive board centering its fund raising efforts around them is a bit like hunting rabbits with a howitzer--a lot of wasted power with minimal results.

To bring in large amounts of money, your board will have to learn about annual and capital campaigns, planned giving, endowment funds and profitable special events-- all of which I cover later in this manual!

The first big step: Commit yourself to fund raising!

Before you do anything else, you and all your fellow board members must make a firm commitment to your nonprofit's fund raising efforts. Just as being a board member means attending meetings and formulating policies, it also means actively taking part in fund raising.

And fund raising is more than watching "other people" raise money and support for your nonprofit--it takes a major commitment of time and effort to make it happen. Read about one board member's awakening...

When Gene Getchell (Lexington, KY) became a member of a nonprofit board, he thought fund raising was sitting back and tallying up the donations as they came rolling in.

"Boy, was I wrong!" Getchell says. "Nobody told me I had to donate myself or ask for money from anyone else. I just thought that people would want to contribute to us because our nonprofit performs such a worthwhile service!"

Getchell and his fellow board members soon found themselves face-to-face with the tough facts of economic life. "We couldn't pay the bills, so we sat down and tackled the budget line by line to find out where the money comes from," he tells me. The exercise was educational, says Getchell. "To raise money, you have to really know where you stand. If you don't, it's like pushing a rope uphill."

Once board members realized it was up to them to raise the money to keep their nonprofit operating, they started making plans. "We set a dollar amount and broke it down into monthly figures so we could see how far we had to go to reach our goal," Getchell says.

"Now we're putting together a master list of people we can solicit--something we hadn't done before. We're also recruiting people to our board who have fund raising ability and we're busy organizing several special events."

<u>Since the board began giving serious attention to fund raising, Getchell says, his nonprofit has made progress in solving its money problems</u>. "I think we're really getting some good things done. We're six months into our fiscal year and we're already ahead of what we raised all of last year!"

Your wildest dreams can come true!

Now that you've determined you really do need to get involved with raising the money your nonprofit needs to keep afloat, you're ready to start thinking about what projects and plans your nonprofit needs funding for.

As a board, do some dreaming about what you'd like to see happen at the nonprofit. Think <u>big</u>! Consider what would help your nonprofit provide even better service to your community. Have each member come up with a "wish list" for your nonprofit.

If you really apply yourself, you'll come up with a list of dreams for your nonprofit that's just as long as a child's birthday list! Your list could include ideas such as new facilities and programs, staff salary raises, major equipment purchases or an endowment to retire your nonprofit's debt.

Don't worry now about how you're going to pay for your "impossible dreams"--just get the things you want for your nonprofit down on paper. I suggest taping a large piece of butcher's paper to a wall where everyone can see it.

Have one board member write the other board members' dreams down. The only rule of this exercise is to remember that no wish or dream is too farfetched.

Once you've committed dreams to paper, it's time to start prioritizing your ideas! Start the process by focusing on those goals you consider really important for your nonprofit. If you've created a list that's truly a mile long, you'll quickly see that you can't do everything at once--but you will be able to get to everything with enough time and money!

Using your wish list as a guide, determine your nonprofit's five top funding needs. Be as specific as you can in describing each goal. Write a rationale to explain how each item benefits your nonprofit. You can use the chart on Page 6 to help you record your priorities.

Grab a piece of the $818 million charitable contribution pie!

Now that you've uncovered your nonprofits's top needs, all that's left to do is come up with the money to pay for them. What's that you say? You think it's an impossible task--that in these hard economic times there's no money to be found for projects like yours?

Think again! Despite all the moaning and groaning about our faltering economy, nearly $818 million is donated to nonprofits in the US every day! (Source: The Funding Center, Alexandria, VA) Here's how this figure breaks down:

Every working day of the year, $818 million is given away in the US!
Foundations give away......................$ 31 million
Corporations give away......................$ 20 million
Governments (federal, state and local) give away..................$367 million
Individuals give away........................$400 million
Total...*$818 million*

Now go back and look at the list of things you want for your nonprofit--and make up your mind to get your share of these charitable dollars! You're off to a good start by working through this manual. Stick with it, read it carefully and you'll learn how to help your nonprofit realize its funding dreams!

Top Funding Needs For Our Nonprofit

#1 Funding Need: _____   _____

_____   _____

_____   _____

_____   _____

#2 Funding Need: _____   _____

_____   _____

_____   _____

_____   _____

#3 Funding Need: _____   _____

_____   _____

_____   _____

_____   _____

#4 Funding Need: _____   _____

_____   _____

_____   _____

_____   _____

#5 Funding Need: _____   _____

_____   _____

_____   _____

_____   _____

CHAPTER 2

How to put together a first-rate fund raising team

Know the key players on your fund raising team..........8
Have board members sign a commitment form.............10
Committees: Where should you begin?..........................11
Former board members are a great resource..................14

Everyone knows that you don't learn to swim by jumping into the deep end of a swimming pool. You need lessons from a qualified instructor first. The same thing applies to learning the how-to's of fund raising.

<u>Take some time now to learn from the experience of board members and administrators who are already successful fund raisers</u>. This way, you'll be ready to swim--not sink--when you begin that all-important work of raising money and support for your nonprofit!

Know the key players on your fund raising team

Like any other collective effort, fund raising requires teamwork. This means that you should know what an individual board member's role is--and play it to the best of your ability! Plus, you need to know how the board as a whole figures into the fund raising process.

There are other <u>key players</u> on your fund raising team whose roles you also must understand. They are: your administrator, director of development and board committees. Here's what each is responsible for:

1) The administrator

When you're in the process of organizing your fund raising plans, don't leave out your administrator. He or she is probably the most up-to-date on exactly what type of funds your nonprofit needs, how much is needed and where to get it.

Because fund raising is a management function, your administrator is the one who is ultimately in charge of fund raising efforts.

The administrator's duties should include:
* outlining funding needs * coordinating overall fund raising strategy * keeping the board informed and up-to-speed on needs and ways to meet them * being visible to the public to create an atmosphere of support * working directly with the board to develop fund raising strategies and activities as needed * working directly with donor groups to solicit money and support * overseeing and controlling the fund raising budget

2) Your development director

If your nonprofit has a development director on staff reporting to the administrator, that person will be the leader of your fund raising efforts.

His or her duties should include:
* developing fund raising strategies and activities to be undertaken by the board * cultivating funding sources * coordinating fund raising activities as needed * charting progress on fund raising activities * acting as a fund raising consultant and coach to the board * reporting to the administrator on the campaign's progress

3) Board committees

One of the first lessons every board member learns is that committees are where the majority of work is done. And you'll find that fund raising is no exception.

Without committees to coordinate fund raising activities, there's usually a lot of talk but precious little action!

Duties of committees should include:
* overseeing specialized aspects of fund raising strategies * implementing fund raising plans drawn up by your administrator, development director or the board as a whole * targeting and contacting donor groups to ask for money and support * acting as advisors to other board members in fund raising activities * conducting and participating in specific fund raising events as needed

Because committees are so vital to successful fund raising, I'll include more details on them later in this chapter.

4) Your board as a whole

Your function as a fund raising body is to assist and support your nonprofit's administrator or development director.

Here's a broader way of looking at it: A board performs two essential roles at a nonprofit. Members are both policy-makers and volunteer consultants to the administrator.

In most instances, you and fellow board members act in a policy-making role. You shape the direction in which your nonprofit will move and delegate authority to your administrator to see that your wishes are carried out.

<u>With fund raising, however, your role is a bit different. As board members, you're expected to actually go out and raise money</u>.

Your role as fund raising consultant means you're like a professional contracted by your nonprofit. This means that you're actually under the "supervision" of your administrator or development director.

> The full board's duties include:
>
> * approve all board fund raising plans
> * brainstorm ways to fulfill board fund raising obligations
> * compile donor lists and strategies for reaching these prospects
> * share expertise whenever called upon to do so
> * participate in all fund raising plans and activities
> * fulfill personal "give and get" goals (see worksheet on a Page 12)

5) Individual board members

Every member of your board should be involved in fund raising, for the simple reason that he or she has a unique contribution to make.

These contributions can be made in any number of ways. For example, board members are an excellent source for donor contacts and ideas for fund raisers. Perhaps more importantly, they give freely of their time, labor and money to your nonprofit.

Even though they don't usually receive a lot of recognition for it, board members are the ones who make fund raising all come together in the end! There's an important rule, however, that all board members should know by heart. It's called the "Three G's" and it stands for

> * **Give**--it's essential that you give personally to fund raising efforts. Your private donation sets an example for potential donors by demonstrating that your commitment to your nonprofit is sincere.
> * **Get**--you need to get money and support from others for your nonprofit.
> * **Get off**--if you can't fulfill these two qualifications, then you need to get off your board. Your nonprofit needs someone who will aggressively work to bring in money!

Have board members sign a commitment form

It's a good idea to emphasize your board's role in fund raising by having each of your board members sign a commitment form for his or her personal "give" and "get" goals.

Administrator Linda Reppond (Seattle, WA) tells me her board's personal contributions and fund raising took off after she asked them to sign a commitment form.

The form outlines the fund raising duties of board members and asks members to list how much they plan to contribute to the nonprofit. It also asks how much their companies will give and how much board members plan to solicit for the nonprofit's annual fund raising event.

"Signing the form strengthens each board member's level of personal commitment,"

Reppond says. "The first year we used the form, 80% of the board contributed $1,000 or more, a big increase over the previous year. Corporate donations are also on the upswing as a result of listing them on the form."

I've included a sample commitment form on Page 12 that you can have all board members sign to show their support of your nonprofit.

Committees: Where should you begin?

A good first step in your fund raising efforts is to set up a board development committee. The purpose of this group is to give fund raising leadership to other board members and subcommittees.

If possible, it should be made up of members with either fund raising experience or solid connections to the professional or business communities in your area.

Administrator Sharon Stetz (Salt Lake City, UT) says her board development committee has been a real force behind her board's successful fund raising efforts.

"We have a development director, but that person's job is to cultivate funding sources and lend professional expertise to the board's overall fund raising efforts," she says.

"Our development committee operates on another level--committee members help fellow board members improve their fund raising know-how and skill.

"For example, committee members have a regular agenda item at board meetings. They use this to give the board updates on current projects and to discuss ideas for future fund raising efforts," Stetz tells me.

If your nonprofit chooses to set up a development committee, you'll want to be sure it stays focused on its fund raising leadership role. An effective way to do this is to write a job description for it.

This document should be similar to one you would write for an administrator. (I've included a sample job description for a development committee on a Page 13).

Once your fund raising efforts grow and develop, you may find that several subcommittees--either in addition to or in place of your development committee--better suit your nonprofit's needs.

One effective way to begin setting up subcommittees is to form them around your specialized areas of fund raising. For example, you might want one committee to focus solely on corporate campaigns. Other committees you might want to add could be a community group committee to encourage service clubs to donate money to your nonprofit, a planned giving committee to secure bequests, trusts and life insurance gifts, and an annual event committee to organize your special fund raising event.

Give and Get Commitment Form

Board member's name: _____

My personal "giving" goal:

I personally pledge $ _____ to this organization to support our fund raising objective.

    I would prefer to make: (please check)
    ( ) One yearly payment
    ( ) Quarterly payments of $ _____
    ( ) Monthly payments of $ _____
    ( ) Weekly payments of $ _____

(Rule of thumb: Each board member should give what he or she can. Some board members will be able to give more than others. But no matter what the amount you can give, it is important to set a giving example!)

My goal for "getting" donations:

As a board member I will personally get (raise) $ _____ from outside sources.

I will solicit $ _____ for our special fund raising event.

I will assist in building our donor list by submitting a total of _____ potential new donors.

I agree to participate in other fund raising activities as needed. I accept this commitment as an understanding of my responsibilities as a board member.

_____
Board member signature

When you have the form signed, pass the information on to your administrator. He or she can then total up all the amounts for the entire board. Once you receive the totals, take a minute and fill out the blanks below. Then sit back and consider what a difference this money will make for your nonprofit!

If each board member meets his/her goal, the total raised will be:

1) Total amount donated by board members $ _____

2) Total amount raised by board members $ _____

Total amount raised by board "giving" and "getting" $ _____

Job Description for a Development Committee

The purpose of a funding development committee is to lead the board in efforts to attract money and services that are necessary to carry out the mission of the organization.

The duties of the board development committee are to:

✓ *Define the short-term and long-term funding needs of this organization with the help of the full board and administrator.* Funding appeals will be ineffective if we can't tell prospective donors exactly what our nonprofit needs the money for.

✓ *Train the full board.* Little training is required to hold a modest fund raising event--but most nonprofits need far more money than small events raise. The committee must become knowledgeable about planned giving, corporate solicitation, lobbying government bodies, grant-writing and marketing.

✓ *Involve all board members in fund raising.* Each board member has the responsibility to do all he or she can to raise money for your nonprofit. The development committee must organize fund raising activities to take into consideration each board member's unique talents.

✓ *Review progress on fund raising goals--and inspire the full board.* The committee must not only report on the status of fund raising efforts, it must be coach and cheerleader to the entire fund raising team.

✓ *Make personal financial donations--and encourage your fellow board members to do likewise.* The best way to convince members of your community to give is to lead by example. Donations by the committee and other board members demonstrate that we believe enough in our nonprofit's mission to put our money where our mouths are.

✓ *Identify, cultivate and enlist community leaders to serve on the funding development committee.* There may be a reservoir of untapped fund raising talent in our community. The committee is responsible for finding it and putting it to good use.

Former board members are a great resource

As you can see, your board members are going to be plenty busy as they get more and more involved with their committee and subcommittee work. To avoid spreading them too thin, you might want to call in some reinforcements--volunteers who can lend their ideas, support and energy.

Luckily, you have a wonderful source of these reinforcements right at your fingertips: former board members!

Former board members are better than money in the bank. They're knowledgeable and committed, and they can usually be counted on to help out, give useful advice and make personal donations.

"Once you've demonstrated dedication to a nonprofit, it's hard to just turn off the switch," says former Board Member John Zelenak (Port Huron, MI). "The desire is still there to make your nonprofit better than ever."

When he retired as an active board member, Zelenak joined his organization's "Past Presidents Council," made up of former board presidents who continue to give expertise. "You could say that we've already learned the ropes--and we can devote our time exclusively to fund raising," he says.

Even without a formal group, your organization can keep former board members involved and committed in fund raising. For example, Administrator Jennifer Reynolds (Boulder, CO) came up with an excellent solution to her "ex-member" problem. Here's her story...

"Not long ago, I lost an excellent fund raiser when his board term expired," she tells me. "I had to figure out ways to keep members like him actively involved with our nonprofit. So I asked him if he'd be willing to continue running one major fund raising project for us and make a couple fund raising calls. He said 'yes' to both.

"Now I ask members leaving the board what they'll continue to do for us--and I keep a file of all that information," Reynolds says. "Even board members who resign usually don't mind helping. Often their reason for resigning was simply because they couldn't make the commitment of time required to be an effective board member."

CHAPTER 3

Use your personal connections to find donors and dollars

How to find prospective donors..16
Use index cards to record data on prospects..........................21

The simplest way to get the fund raising ball rolling is for each member of your board to ask friends, relatives or business associates for donations. By soliciting those they know first, your board members can gradually "warm up" to asking people for money.

Before you start making calls, you need to do some work as a board. Hold a brainstorming session and have board members compile lists of potential donors from people they know.

Now combine the lists and decide which board member is best suited to solicit each prospective donor. Try to make the best fit!

Things to look for in matching members to donors are similar professional backgrounds, avocational interests, age, religious affiliation, or membership in civic, fraternal or other organizations.

Matching a board member with a donor prospect makes it easier for each individual member to ask for contributions. That's because shared interests or similar backgrounds are an effective conversational icebreaker during solicitation calls.

I've included in this chapter a number of tips to help you gather the names of potential donors for your nonprofit. Take some time now to study these pointers--I think you'll find them very useful!

How to find prospective donors

Fund raising is a "percentages" game: The larger the list of potential donors a nonprofit can acquire, the better its chances of bringing in more money and more large donations! The key to this, of course, is finding those potential donors.

A professional fund raiser with more than 30 years experience says many people are waiting to donate to nonprofits. Incredible as it may sound, they often end up not giving anything.

"They don't contribute for a simple reason: No one from a nonprofit ever came around and explained to them how they could have helped out," he tells me.

Here is this professional's advice for pinpointing potential donors:

1) Make a list of your personal friends and acquaintances.

I know this could be lengthy, but don't leave anyone off.

Once you've compiled a master list of everyone you know, arrange the donor prospects in order of priority. Place two stars by names likely to make the largest donations. Put one star by those who would probably make a smaller donation.

Leave the names of people on your list blank who you're not sure will make a donation at all.

There's one important point to remember: Your goal is to put together the largest possible pool of donors you can. When you begin making calls, in addition to asking them for money, be sure to ask all three groups for the names of *their* friends or associates who might be interested in giving to your nonprofit.

One final point: Don't write off unmarked names as "hopeless cases," based on your perception of what they're likely to give. You never know who may surprise you with a large donation--or provide you with a name of someone who can!

2) Study the donor lists of other local organizations.

Many nonprofits publish lists of donors--and the amounts they gave--in their newsletters or annual reports. These publications are readily available and often are excellent informational tools for your fund raising efforts!

Another simple way to gain access to potential donors is to exchange donor lists with other nonprofits. Many organizations are willing to do this because they recognize the need to update their own lists by adding new prospects. For an exchange of this type to work, however, both lists must be made up of donors who are likely to contribute to either nonprofit.

To find organizations willing to swap lists, ask your fellow board members if they know any key people at other nonprofits. Once again, have the person acquainted with the other organization's administrator, board president or board member do the asking. And remember: You're not asking for a personal favor--you're seeking something that benefits both nonprofits.

Organizations that might want to exchange donor lists:

3) Read plat books to find out who owns land.

One way to measure a prospect's giving potential is to find out what his or her real estate holdings are. People who own large amounts of valuable land are excellent potential donors to your nonprofit. Someday their estates will go to someone--why not you? The key is to develop a good relationship with them over time.

<u>You can do this by getting to know them personally</u>. If you show a genuine interest in them as individuals, they'll be far more likely to donate to your nonprofit.

One of the best sources of information about people who own large amounts of property is a plat book. Plat books are maps of an area that not only tell you who owns property--but how much and where the land is located. Ask to see the official plat books at your local government office--or ask officials where you can buy inexpensive copies.

Board Member Barry Peacock (Genesee Depot, WI) says he spends hours reading plat books, looking for clues to who might be a good potential donor to his nonprofit.

"I make a point of gathering names of property owners--especially those who own quite a bit of property or who live in well-to-do neighborhoods," he says.

4) Conduct a special mailing to your previous supporters--and ask them for the names of other potential donors.

One of the most valuable sources of new donor prospects is the people who have generously supported your organization over the years. Read how one nonprofit has successfully tapped into this network...

This organization recently mailed letters, with postage-paid return envelopes, to 400 faithful contributors asking them to give the names of their friends and associates who are good donor prospects.

The response was tremendous! Nearly a third returned the letters, <u>resulting in 150 new names</u> for the organization's mailing list!

Once these were added to the nonprofit's list of donor prospects, board members initialed the names of people they knew to show which people they would contact in the future.

If you decide on a special mailing, be sure your board members carefully go over names for those they know personally. Remember, the more you have in common with donor prospects, the better your chances of raising money!

5) People employed at companies with matching gift programs are good prospects to add to your list.

Many companies match employee contributions to nonprofits or charities in their communities. Because some companies double or triple what their employees give, matching programs can be a lucrative source of funding for your nonprofit!

For information about a list of companies that match gifts, contact: Cheryl Martin, Director, National Clearinghouse for Corporate Matching Gift Info, CASE, Ste 400, 11 Dupont Circle, Washington, DC 20036; (202)328-5956.

Martin publishes two lists that are of interest to nonprofits: One names 333 companies that support cultural nonprofits, like museums, symphonies, dance troupes etc; the other, 234 companies that support social service and health organizations.

In addition, Martin's organization will supply a list of corporate donors that sponsor specific types of nonprofits. Simply state what kind of nonprofit you are, and the list will be made. List prices will vary depending on the type of list you request.

6) Identify people who have no apparent heirs.

These are often excellent prospects for estate gifts because they have no close relatives to include in a will.

Church and city directories are good sources to investigate for people who have no heirs or relatives. To help you in your search, look for these basic clues: Advanced age, no listing of children, the number of occupants in a house or use of the courtesy title, "Miss."

Careful reading of directories to find potential donors can be well worth the effort. Consider the case of a Midwestern organization I know that recently received a gift of $100,000 from the estate of a widow with no heirs. The administrator of this nonprofit says he came across the woman's name while looking through church directories for potential donors!

7) Find out who lives in the "wealthy" part of town or who are business owners.

Wouldn't it be a big help to your fund raising efforts to be able to drive through a well-to-do neighborhood--and know the names of the people who live there? You bet it would!

The easiest way to get this information is to buy a directory of your city or town. Directories of communities in the US are published by the R L Polk & Company of Detroit and are available by writing to the company.

These directories list residents by address and give their occupations and phone numbers. They're an excellent "one-stop" source of prospects who have the ability to make large donations!

For more information on Polk City Directories, write or phone: R L Polk & Company, 1155 Brewery Park Blvd, Detroit, MI 48207; (313)393-0880. Directories are published for cities as small as 10,000 and range in price from $50 to $200.

8) Make a list of business people and professionals older than 40.

People in this age group have generally made their way up in the career ladder and are at their highest earning potential. Many have also already reared their children and can afford to make donations to a worthwhile nonprofit.

Name	Pertinent Information	Giving Potential

9) Compile the names of people who know your nonprofit firsthand.

The obvious source for this group of potential donors is the families and friends of the people you serve. And don't forget about those people who regularly volunteer their time to work at your nonprofit!

Name	Pertinent Information	Giving Potential

10) Don't overlook the "sleepers."

These are usually unassuming people who have built up wealth without making a big public display. The best way to find them is to ask around. Do your friends, business acquaintances or fellow board members know of anyone who fits the description of a sleeper?

Name	Pertinent Information	Giving Potential

11) Read the business section of newspapers to learn who has recently sold a business.

These are people coming into a large amount of money--and they often donate to nonprofits as a tax break. The sale of an established business is a prime news story, so be sure to scan your newspaper's business section. Also be on the alert for stories about charitable donations by businesses or corporate foundations. These will give you an idea of what types of nonprofits get funded--and at what levels.

Name	Pertinent Information	Giving Potential

Use index cards to record data on prospects

Once you've matched board members to a potential donor, you want to make sure other members won't call on the same prospect. This way, you'll save yourself a lot of embarrassment--and you won't give donors the impression that your nonprofit is disorganized or uses high-pressure selling tactics.

It's also a good idea to keep your personal donor solicitation schedule well-organized. For example, you'll want to record when and where you plan to meet a prospect, relevant information about his or her background, etc.

Board President Lionel Fallows tells me he records this data in a personal card file of people he solicits for donations. The cards are a handy way for him to quickly recall details about a person's background when it's time to call on a donor or prospect.

I think 3x5 cards work great for this type of index, and they can easily be stored in an inexpensive metal or plastic file. Here's how Fallows (Amsterdam, NY) describes his method of tracking donors and prospects...

"First, I record people's names on their cards, along with the names of spouses or other family members. I include the occupation of donors or prospects and any organizations they belong to," he says.

"I use the cards to refresh my memory. Before I go on a call, I do my homework. For example, if a person is a donor, I write down the amount of the most recent gift. And I make a note of how much I expect to ask the donor for in the future."

Fallow's card file has 80 to 90 names. "If my administrator has given me a specific assignment, like approaching people who can give $5,000 to $10,000 to an equipment project, I sort through my cards and pick likely donors," he says. "I review my files and stick those cards in my coat pocket--just in case I cross paths with one of these people in the course of my daily routine."

The card file also allows Fallows to organize his solicitation schedule. "We solicit people on a three-year rotation," he says. "This means I won't approach donors next year if they've just made a three-year commitment. I go after a new group of prospects, and the file helps me remember whom I've already asked."

Fallow's cards look like this:

Front side

```
Name:

Address:                              Date:

                                      Age:

Phone:                                Occupation:

Spouse's name:                        Spouse's occupation:

Referred by:                          Date of referral:

Previous gift:

Potential gift:
```

Back side

```
Prospect/donor interests:

Organizations he or she belongs to:

Other important information:

Date of first call and results:

Date of second call and results:
```

CHAPTER 4

Use your business connections to uncover money and support for your nonprofit

How can you personally help your organization?.........24
Use your position in the workplace to raise funds........ 26
How your employer can help your nonprofit................ 27
Go after large donations from other corporations......... 28

If you want to raise thousands (or even millions!) for your nonprofit, tap into one of the most logical sources of this money--your own board members' business and corporate connections. The first step in this process is to look carefully at how *your own credentials* can be used to benefit your nonprofit. Take a few minutes to go over the following list to find out where you fit into your organization's fund raising efforts. After each appropriate section, write down how you can contribute.

How can you personally help your organization?

If you are a/an:

{ } *Financial professional*

You can...

Secure financing for your organization, identify potential contributors among clients, suggest that clients donate life insurance policies and advise donors/clients about tax-deductible contributions.

Potential donors are:_____

_____

_____

{ } *Attorney*

Help identify potential donors and suggest that your clients include your organization in their estate plans.

Potential donors are: _____

_____

_____

{ } *Medical professional*

Contribute cash, offer advice on wellness and health insurance, and use your position in the community to influence others to contribute to your organization.

Ideas, potential donors are: _____

_____

_____

| | *Company executive or employee* | Arrange for your company to make contributions of cash/equipment/ inventory, match gifts to your organization made by your employees, and encourage employees to give and become volunteers.

Possible gifts, donors are: _____

_____

_____

| | *Active community volunteer* | Make connections with other community groups. Use your connections for lobbying, cooperative fund raising, and recruiting more volunteers for your organization.

Potential volunteers are: _____

_____

_____

| | *Social worker, educator, clergy* | Use your influence with funding sources or congregations. Suggest ways that your organization might better meet the needs of people you serve. By better meeting needs, more people will want to donate to your nonprofit.

Ideas, potential donors are: _____

_____

_____

| | *Politician* | Exert your personal influence in government, and recommend ways to lobby local, state and federal funding sources.

Ideas are: _____

_____

_____

Use your position in the workplace to raise funds

After you've determined how you can help your nonprofit through your own professional position and connections, it's time to branch out. The best place to start is with your own place of work!

1) Check out your employer's charitable giving policy.

Board Member Beverly Copeland (Pasadena, CA), a corporate public relations specialist, says all board members should have a thorough knowledge of their employer's giving policy.

"<u>Corporations generally give first to nonprofits their employees or retirees support either through donations or volunteer work," she says</u>. "Many employees, however, don't realize their employers have programs to match employee giving. The best way to find out is simply to ask. Often it's just a matter of filling out a form and making a request for money."

According to Copeland, there is an added advantage in reminding your <u>fellow employees</u> about their company's matching gifts policy as well. "It helps you bring in more donations," she says.

"When people know that whatever they give to a local cause will be <u>doubled</u> by their employer, they just seem to dig deeper into their wallets or pocketbooks!"

This doubling of donations can really make a difference for your nonprofit. Just think, you'll receive twice the money for the same effort!!!

2) Can your employer donate services?

Although fund raising is often equated with simply asking for donations of money, your board shouldn't underestimate the value of <u>donated services</u>! Listen to Administrator Daren Busch (Lexington, KY) who's in a position to know...

"We were sitting in a meeting looking at the budget," he tells me. "There was a $2,000 item for printing new brochures. One of our board members is an executive with a corporation in our area. He just piped up, 'My company can handle that.'

"I wrote a memo explaining our printing needs to his corporate headquarters. He forwarded the request, recommending that it be approved. Since then, all the design and printing of our brochures and newsletter is to be done through his corporation's advertising department."

3) Use your business letterhead in fund raising efforts.

Board Chairman Irwin Rosenberg (Glendale, CA) says he uses his company's letterhead to solicit funds from customers and business associates. "Last year, I sent 10 to 20 fund raising letters typed on my business letterhead for our nonprofit's annual awards dinner. This brought in $3,000.

"You get a higher donation rate--from 50% to 70% of those contacted--when you use a company letterhead to ask for donations from other businesses," he says. "The reason is simple: <u>The people you buy from want to stay on your good side</u>, so they contribute to your fund raising project!

"In my business, for example, I buy a lot of supplies and equipment from other companies. Naturally, they want to keep me happy, so they give to our nonprofit's fund raising campaign," Rosenberg says. "One business associate even wrote a $5,000 check for our capital drive. At the same time, he bought two tickets to our awards dinner."

<u>Warning</u>: Before using company stationery for fund raising purposes, be sure your employer approves of the practice.

(Note: The IRS says use of business letterheads and stationery doesn't qualify as a charitable deduction. Such use is considered a business expense because it promotes your business. "Publication 334" discusses business expenses and charitable contributions. Order your free copy by phoning the IRS: 1-800-829-3676.)

How your employer can help your nonprofit

Ideas	How This Could Help	Donation potential

Go after large donations from other corporations

After you've mined your own workplace for contributions, you're ready for another important source of donations--other corporations. Before you get started, however, take awhile to learn some important facts about soliciting corporate donations.

1) Develop a range of corporate giving options.

Some corporations prefer to spread their gifts over time, while others prefer to give a single donation. Generally speaking, you will improve your chances of corporate donations if you can give company executives a range of options. This allows them to choose the giving method that best fits in with their charitable donation policies.

According to Ray Norwood, vice president of public affairs for a large, Seattle-based energy company, his company avoids lengthy donation agreements. "Like a lot of other corporations, we'd rather make a once-only gift of dollars or equipment than commit to a long-term donation," he says.

Norwood adds, however, that other companies may prefer what he calls limited commitments.

"For instance, a three-year pledge would fall into this category.

"These sorts of donations are acceptable because they are limited," he tells me. "Many companies like short-term commitments like these instead of giving piddling amounts each year over a long time. Not being tied to a long-range project frees them to respond to other charitable needs."

Of course, there is always the exception to the rule and you may find corporations that prefer to spread their nonprofit donations over a period of time. This is why it's important to tailor your fund raising options to the needs of each company. You'll find that corporations appreciate the consideration.

Another important point to remember about corporate solicitation is that short-term

---

Solicit from corporations and execs at the same time

When board members of a Raleigh, North Carolina, nonprofit solicit a corporation for a gift, they kill two birds with one stone! That is, they make double sure to ask the corporation's top executive and other influential managers for personal contributions at the same time they ask the company to consider a corporate gift.

Their reasoning is simple: It doubles the donations! Plus, these board members believe that when the CEO is convinced to give personally to their nonprofit, this will influence favorably his or her future decisions on giving corporate money.

The strategy has paid off handsomely! When the nonprofit recently hosted an annual breakfast for 100 corporate leaders, board members handed out two pledge cards--one for the company and one for the CEO.

"Contributions from the executives of those corporations attending are coming in right and left!" reports fund raiser Polly Jenkins. "We started in December and already we have more than $4,000 in personal contributions from them--plus money that their corporations gave."

donations don't have to be small ones. For example, Norwood's company recently donated heating equipment worth $31,000 to a nonprofit. It was a short-term gift--but nothing to sneeze at either!

2) A "personal touch" can make a million-dollar difference.

Development Director Graham Thomas' organization recently received several corporate gifts ranging from $7,500 to $250,000. Nine of these were $50,000 or greater--and six others were more than $25,000!

How did his nonprofit attract this kind of corporate generosity? According to Thomas, it was his board's "personal approach."

Board fund raising teams--themselves made up of corporate executives--hand delivered a businesslike solicitation proposal to each corporate prospect.

Aside from things like the nonprofit's background and material on its current campaign, each copy of the proposal featured a cover letter personally addressed to the corporate executive. According to Thomas, CEOs appreciate the fact that they rate special attention.

Thomas also says his board members invited prospects to breakfast and a tour of their facility. The tours were a very effective part of his nonprofit's personal approach to seeking corporate gifts, he adds.

"I call it the 'touch and feel' approach to fund raising. The tours and breakfasts give donor prospects firsthand knowledge of what we're all about. This introduction to our nonprofit often sparks a personal commitment," he says.

For example, the executive of a financial institution who toured the nonprofit later attended a performance of the organization's youth theater. The result was a $50,000 corporate gift--and a $25,000 personal gift from the executive!

3) Board gives donors something in return!

Board members at a California nonprofit have found an innovative way to keep business gifts coming in year after year: They give companies something in return for their donations.

Here's how it works...

"We created a Business Coalition,'" explains Board Member Kristy Gregg (San Diego, CA). "Companies buy 'memberships' ranging from $1,000 to $25,000. Depending on the size of their gift, we provide each company with specific services in return for their generosity."

For example, Gregg's nonprofit offers counseling services at no charge to one corporate donor's employees. Other donors get a free public relations services that lets the public know they are supporting a worthy cause.

"We may print the company's name and logo in our quarterly newsletter, which is mailed to 10,000 homes," Gregg says.

"Companies may also be listed in the program for our annual fund raiser, or they may be included on our donor recognition wall or given a corporate support plaque. Finally, if the contribution is large enough, we'll put out a media release to make sure the news gets out."

<u>According to Gregg, the local business community has responded enthusiastically to her nonprofit's "Business Coalition."</u> "I think they really appreciate the fact that we're willing to give them something valuable in return for their generous support," she says. "It's also a unique approach--no other nonprofit in our area uses it. So we stand out in the crowd of organizations asking for money."

CHAPTER 5

Asking donors for money

Be thoroughly prepared for the first call......................... 32
Don't underestimate the power of "named" gifts..........33
What named gifts can you offer donors?........................ 35
Practice on friends before you solicit strangers..............36
How much should you ask a donor to give?................... 36
Last-minute reminders before you make a call.............. 37
Carefully plan your meetings with donors..................... 38
Whom should I include on my meetings schedule?...... 39
Board members bring "golden touch" to
      fund raising letters.. 40
Outline what your fund raising letter might say........... 41
Who are the best prospects to receive this letter?.......... 41

Let's face it--not many people actually enjoy the thought of asking for money. It's a <u>natural fear</u>, but board members everywhere have also overcome it and gone on to become successful fund raisers.

How did they manage to do this? They simply realized that very few of us were born with the talent to go out and raise a million dollars at a single crack! The key is to approach fund raising like you would any other job--by preparing yourself to meet all aspects of it!

You need to have a thorough understanding of your nonprofit's services, a clear picture of how donations will be used and a good sense of what every prospect can afford to give.

Be thoroughly prepared before the first call

Perhaps the single most important piece of information you can offer prospects is how your nonprofit benefits your community. If you can't convince potential donors that your cause is extremely valuable, they won't give you the time of day-- much less a cash donation!

<u>So, before you begin meeting with prospective contributors, make sure you can clearly explain precisely what your nonprofit does</u>. You can have this information at your fingertips by writing a statement defining your nonprofit and its services.

Most nonprofits call this a vision statement because it explains what they stand for and what their nonprofit has the potential to become. A vision statement will help your board members answer questions from potential donors. Attractively printed statements are also excellent promotional materials to hand out during solicitation calls.

> Here's what you should include in your nonprofit's vision statement:
>
> * The importance of your activities and programs
> * Who benefits from your services
> * Your philosophy of service
> * Opportunities you see for greater service
> * How more funds will help your nonprofit grow and expand

Once you and your fellow board members have agreed on what these things mean, find an experienced writer to put them down on paper. Maybe a board member, staffer or a volunteer could fill this role. Make sure you recruit someone with the required skill--you want this statement to make a favorable first impression!

Here are several things to keep in mind during the writing stage:

● *Make your statement "reader comfortable."* Don't use technical or highly charged language. Just state your nonprofit's case by giving the essential information about its services and how the donor's help is needed.

● *Keep it brief.* Your readers won't be any more impressed by five pages than they will be by one--especially when the single-page statement is informative and skillfully written. So do some editorial honing!

● *Have your board approve the statement.* Once a draft is complete, have board members review and discuss it. Be sure to review the statement periodically after your board has approved it. This way you'll keep it updated and ready to hand out to potential donors anytime.

● *Put it to good use!* Now that you have a document stating your purpose and your needs, don't let it gather dust on a shelf somewhere. Give copies to your board members and instruct them to pass them out whenever they meet potential donors!

On the following page, you'll find a vision statement put together by Administrator Bob Mather (Pittsburgh, PA). Take a look at how he has crafted his statement to include all the necessary information.

Besides being able to discuss your nonprofit's activities, you'll also need to explain what you need additional funding for. In the wake of the recent United Way of America scandal, <u>donors want assurances that their donations will be used properly</u>. So be prepared to outline your plans for the contribution--whether it is to expand services, meet operating expenses, purchase new equipment or expand your facility.

It's very important that you answer questions about where the money goes calmly and thoroughly. If you don't, the prospect may decide not to give or--worse yet--put so many restrictions on his or her gift that it becomes virtually worthless. Case in point...

I recently heard about a nonprofit board in Maine who had received a tidy $12,000 gift. But, to ensure that the funds weren't misused, the donor attached one huge string: The money could be used only to buy coffee and donuts for board meetings!

The result: Board members ate well--as they continued to watch their nonprofit struggle to meet necessary expenses like payroll and routine building maintenance.

Moral of the story: Reassure donors that their money will be well spent (and make sure it is!) and then ask them for "unrestricted" gifts. This gives you and your administrator the control you need to use the funds where they will do the most good.

Don't underestimate the power of "named" gifts

Experienced fund raisers will tell you that one of the most effective ways to convince prospects to contribute is to name something after the donor. These named gifts can range from a wing on a new building to a brick in a new sidewalk.

Vision Statement for the Vocational Rehabilitation Center

Through the years, Vocational Rehabilitation Center's mission as a nonprofit service organization has remained constant--to provide the highest quality services to assist people with disabling conditions to enter the work force and become productive, wage-earning citizens. VRC clients are referred to VRC for vocational rehabilitation and training primarily by the Pennsylvania State Office of Vocational Rehabilitation and the Allegheny County Mental Health/Mental Retardation Office. Fees for services to these clients are paid to VRC by the referring agency. Currently, VRC also serves 26 disabled client workers without training monies.

Beyond client fees from the referring agencies, income is generated by the products and services produced by the clients themselves in the Agency's workshops. These work centers, at both Pittsburgh and Mon Valley Branch, provide paid work to our clients. Clients receive training and work experiences in such tasks as manufacturing, printing, janitorial and building maintenance, mailing, microfilming and packaging. The tasks range from simple assembly to the complex manufacturing of a fluorescent desk lamp for the federal government. Nearly $1.3 million of revenue to VRC is generated annually by clients in the workshops.

VRC clients include those who are developmentally and physically disabled, those with chronic mental health problems, visual and hearing impairments, and those with autism and learning disabilities. VRC also serves clients with problems arising from heart disease, arthritis, head trauma, and alcohol and drug abuse. According to the 1980 Census, the developmentally disabled and physically disabled in Pittsburgh alone numbered almost 68,000 and in Allegheny County the number increased to almost 232,000. These figures did not include drug and alcohol abusers who were eligible for the services provided by VRC.

The agency's masthead motto, "Bringing people and the workplace together," at once summarizes VRC's goal and is a testimony to its success. In 1989, 70% of the people served by VRC reached higher, less restrictive vocational goals. Of those who completed the Placement Program, 81% were employed. Since 1980, more than 2,200 disabled persons have been placed in competitive employment. Their income ranges from minimum wage to more than $40,000 per year. It is estimated that this new work force will earn almost two million dollars in wages each year and save taxpayers more than $300,000 yearly in public assistance money. Overall, it is estimated that every dollar spent by VRC in placing a person is returned to the community tenfold via taxes generated and a reduction in the need for public assistance.

Administrator Michail Moran tells me that named giving is a very effective fund raising strategy because it gives donors something "in return" for their generosity.

"For this reason, named gifts are a very profitable way for nonprofits to raise funds," he says. "People just tend to give more if they know they'll be publicly recognized!"

Here are three profitable named gift programs you'll want to investigate...

● *Major building projects.* A few years ago, a Greensburg, Pennsylvania, hospital established a named gift program to fund a remodeling project. Donors were given the chance to have a new room named after themselves. The program has generated more than $400,000 in donations.

A brochure, which featured architectural drawings of the building additions, was used to market the named gift program. It was mailed to past and prospective donors, and listed the prices for each new room. The brochure provided an added attraction: A schedule that allows donors to spread "payments" of their gift over time. For example, naming a library costs $5,000, which could be paid quarterly in $250 increments over five years.

● *New, unnamed streets in your community.* Development Director Dennis Donin (Portland, OR) "immortalizes" the names of donors on street signs in new housing areas.

For instance, one year his organization auctioned off the naming of three new streets, bringing in $1,800. The following year, Donin honored the top pledge collector in his annual walkathon with a street name. Contact county surveyors, city planners, local development companies and housing companies to find out about new streets in your community. Be sure you look into local ordinances governing street naming.

● *A "Walk of Fame" named gift program.* Bring a touch of Hollywood to your community! Administrator Diana Smalley (Edmond, OK) gives donors a chance to put their names on walkway bricks.

Donors can choose from two options: $100 "executive" bricks in the entry of a new building or $40 "booster" bricks, which are part of the nearby sidewalk. This is a great fund raising idea, because it's limited only by the number of bricks in your new building project!

What named gifts can you offer donors?

Practice on friends before you solicit strangers

Let's say your board members are still not comfortable with the prospect of actually having to go out and ask for donations. Take a tip from Administrator Cindy Miller, who's come up with a great idea to help her board get their fund raising feet wet...

Miller (Palo Alto, CA) has each board member polish his or her "asking" skills by first soliciting other board members.

This strategy accomplishes three important things, Miller tells me. "First, it gives board members a chance to practice asking for money," she says. "Second, it's really a true solicitation call because a donation is expected.

"Third and perhaps most important, it puts board members in the shoes of donors to our nonprofit. Board members can know firsthand how it feels to be asked for money," she says. "This helps them understand that you should always approach a donor in the same way you would want to be asked."

How much should you ask a donor to give?

When you asked a fellow board member for a donation, were you prepared to ask for a specific amount? You should have been, because knowing how much to ask for is an important part of fund raising! Here's why:

Incredible as it sounds, you can inadvertently ask for a donation so small that it insults the donor! Read about how one nonprofit board member learned this the hard way...

He tells me that asking donors for less than they're prepared to give can be a disaster. Not long ago, this board member called on a wealthy potential donor and asked for a $250 donation. The donor took a check out of his pocket and ripped it up saying, "Well, I guess you won't be needing this contribution for $2,500 then."

Without a doubt you want to avoid alienating donors by asking for too little. And so it's sometimes a good practice to "overshoot" the amount you really expect a person to give.

Read what this New York nonprofit development director has to say...

"It's almost a psychological law," she explains. "If you ask a prospective donor for a sum that is higher than you know he or she can contribute, you'll often get a larger donation than you would have normally expected.

"This is because it's flattering to the donor prospect that you think he or she is well-off enough to make a large gift. Naturally, that person wants you to continue thinking that way--so he or she gives more!" she says.

On the other hand, asking for a donation that grossly overshoots your mark will likely turn off a potential donor. He or she will be convinced that you're just plain out of touch with reality. Here are a couple of tips to help you know exactly how much you should ask for...

1) Find out how much prospects give to other nonprofits.

Often this information is published in organizational newsletters or annual reports. If a donor has given to programs like yours, the chances are that he or she will contribute to your nonprofit--in similar amounts.

2) Conduct a survey of your donors.

Vice President for Annual Giving Jacqulyn Muller (Everett, WA) recently sent donors a one-page questionnaire. It asked for the donor's occupation/employer, spouse's occupation/employer, church affiliation and service/civic club memberships.

"Knowing a donor's occupation and that of his or her spouse, plus this other information, helps us know what to ask for when we make solicitation calls," says Muller.

Last-minute reminders before you make a call

Administrator Susan Church (Okemos, MI) has passed some tips on to me about making effective donor calls. They make a great, last-minute checklist of things to think about before you actually begin soliciting.

Church does a great job of getting her board members started on fund raising, so read carefully what she has to say:

● *Set the tone of the meeting by beginning with a compliment.* "You might say, 'I know you give generously to many important causes. That's why I hope that this year you'll consider giving to my nonprofit which does....'" she says.

This approach accomplishes three things, she adds. First, it makes the donor prospect feel good because you're acknowledging his or her generosity. Second, you've explained the services your nonprofit performs. Finally, you've tied the donor's special interests to the contribution you want him or her to make.

● *Try to relate what you like about your nonprofit to the interests of each donor.* "You can talk more effectively to people about something that grabs your interest. And the chances are that your enthusiasm will excite the donor's interest," Church says.
"You don't have to be a walking encyclopedia. Just talk about your favorite programs and how a gift can help make them even better."

● *Know when to be quiet.* "This is a tough one, even for me," Church laughs. "After you've told a donor prospect how much of a gift you hope he or she gives--it's time to shut up.

"Just look the person in the eye, and smile. The donor won't take very long to react. After all, nobody's going to stare back at you for five minutes. Let the next word come from the prospect--and you'll know where you stand."

● *Mentally work through the "worst case scenario."* Board members can easily become obsessed by the possibility that a prospect may turn them down. As a fund raiser, you can expect to be turned down--it's just part of the job. But you should also know how to turn rejection around...

"If people say they're not interested in giving you money, let them know that you respect their decision," Church says. "But also be sure to tell them that you'd still like to explain your nonprofit's services.

"Promise not to talk about money. Your visit then becomes an opportunity to explain your nonprofit's mission--and that's OK. You've just laid the groundwork for future solicitations."

Carefully plan your meetings with donors

You've reviewed in your mind the key points of your first solicitation call. Now all you need is to pick a place to meet the donor prospect! I suggest that you choose a setting where both of you will feel comfortable. This might be lunch at a restaurant, an informal meeting at your house or the donor's, or maybe even having coffee in your prospect's office.

Whatever you decide, here are some important points about "donor psychology" that you need to be aware of...

1) Donors give to people they know, like and trust.

Remember, a warm personality "sells" better than cold facts. Be yourself, keep your meeting personal and spend some time getting to know the donor.

2) Play up interests you share with the donor.

If you've carefully matched board members with prospects, you have more in common with this person than any other board member. So chat up your common interests!

You're more likely to get a donation if you come across as interested in the same things the prospect is.

3) Let the donor "have the floor."

After you've broken the ice conversationally, let the prospect do most of the talking. You need to be taking mental notes about this individual's enthusiasm and interest in your nonprofit's programs.

4) Know ahead of time what you want to accomplish.

Obviously, you want a generous donation at the end of the meeting. But you're also looking for other individual and corporate donor prospects. Make a note before your meeting to ask the donor if he or she knows of another source who would be willing to help your nonprofit. Don't be afraid to ask the donor if he or she can set up a meeting between you and this source.

<u>Action</u>: Plan several meetings with donor prospects for the month ahead. Arrange the first few meetings with the most influential people on your list. Ask them for prospect leads and then follow up!

Whom should I include on my meetings schedule?

Name	Information	Meeting Date

Board members bring "golden touch" to fund raising letters

If the thought of making your first personal solicitation is just too much for you to handle, try doing it by letter. Although a fund raising letter is less effective than a face-to-face meeting, it's better than nothing!

Before you write any letters, there are two important things to remember. First, donors like to feel that they're receiving special treatment, so make your letters as personal as possible. Second, take advantage of your contacts in the business or professional community--you can make a more persuasive case for your nonprofit if a prospect knows you and is willing to make a donation to a nonprofit you support.

Here's how successful fund raisers have made these letter-writing tips work for them...

● Administrator Judith Kasser (Boston, MA) says her organization brought in an extra $10,000--all because board members applied the personal touch to their letter-writing campaign.

Kasser's nonprofit had traditionally raised money through the mail--by sending a form letter to all prospects. One year, her board decided it was time to try a new twist. Each member supplied five or six names of friends and business contacts. The nonprofit's public relations staffers wrote a fund raising letter, and board members personally signed letters sent to their friends.

"We sent out fewer than half the letters we'd sent out before," says Kasser, "but the personal letters from board members were what produced the $10,000 increase in donations we received."

● Board Member John Howard (Phoenix, AZ) tells me that he emphasizes his strong commitment to the nonprofit's mission in personal letters to prospects.

"The real secret is to convince donors that I really believe in the cause I'm asking them to support," he says. "This gives the letter-writing campaign its credibility and gets them to contribute."

Howard also uses his own word processor to write a letter to each person on his organization's donor list. His successful response rate has been as high as 98%!

● Administrator Chris Spence (Abilene, TX) says his board members add a short, handwritten message to letters sent to prospects they know. "Our board members have numerous contacts in the community--and we've found that this personal touch really pays off," he says.

● Board Member Wilma Askinas (Great Neck, NY) has discovered an inexpensive way to reach thousands of readers in her community: She writes "letters to the editor" to encourage the public to give to her organization.

In fact, Askinas says one letter appeared in the *New York Times.* If Askinas can publish her letter in one of the world's greatest newspapers, you should have a good shot at getting your organization's views and needs in your local paper!

A word of caution: Before you mail your letter, run it past your administrator and the rest of the board to make sure it is consistent with your organization's goals and policies.

Outline what your fund raising letter might say

1) What will get a donor's attention?

2) What funding need will most appeal to donors?

3) What kind of action/donation will you ask donors to make?

Who are the best prospects to receive this letter?

List all people here:

List professional writers who might critique this letter for you:

CHAPTER 6

Make your special event outstanding in every way

Consider successful events other nonprofits have used 44
How to be sure your event will make money 46
Maximize profits from your fund raising events 46
Business sponsors can guarantee a profitable event 48

Special fund raising events are fun to plan and hold. They also bring in that extra cash your nonprofit often needs to keep its head above water in troubled financial times.

But keep in mind that yours is not the only organization planning a special event--the competition for community support is intense. If your event is going to be a moneymaker, you need to make sure it stands out from the crowd. And that is sometimes easier said than done.

<u>With the help of this chapter, you'll find out how to make sure your new events will truly be moneymakers and how to rejuvenate your old events so they're more successful than they've ever been in the past.</u>

Don't kid yourself: A profitable special event will take lots of work. You'll probably need more hands than those of your fellow board members to help out. Committees are vital to the success of an event--and we'll talk about effective committee structure later in this chapter.

So let's get started. To get your creative juices flowing, take a look at what events other nonprofits have used to raise dollars and support for their nonprofit...

Consider successful events other nonprofits have used

Here are just a few of the literally hundreds of successful fund raising events that nonprofits have used:

● *Collecting pennies.* A nonprofit board in Iowa raised $10,000 from plastic collection cups it distributed to community businesses. A large Plexiglas container for donations of pennies (nickels, dimes, quarters also accepted!) at a local mall served as the "focal point" for the fund raiser.

● *Tour of homes.* Do your board members or nonprofit supporters live in houses that people are dying to see? Try arranging a tour of these homes on a Sunday afternoon and charge admission to the public. Owners love to explain the history and architectural style of their houses. Board members tell me the tours are an excellent way to raise money with no overhead (no word play intended!).

● *International beer-tasting festival.* Try this variation of the common wine-and-cheese party that a board member from Massachusetts came up with. She went around her community asking liquor stores for samples of imported beers.

Tables were then set up at the nonprofit featuring beer and snacks appropriate to the country where the beer was brewed. For an entrance fee, participants sampled beer and food to their hearts' content!

Or try a chocolate extravaganza. This event is similar to the beer-tasting festival, only candy-makers in your area supply goodies for participants to eat.

● *Roasting the mayor.* Here's a good idea for your annual fund raising dinner that's sure to pack them in. Instead of the usual after-dinner speeches, try some homegrown hilarity. Have prominent citizens poke fun (offer to help with your writing talent) at your community's mayor.

Other ideas for fund raisers are: Balloon shows, popcorn sales, bike tours, wishing wells, cook-offs and bake-offs...the possibilities are limited only by your board's imagination.

Why not hold a board brainstorming session to come up with fun ideas for special events? Just start writing them down as they come into your head.

Event Idea	Description	How Much Could You Raise?

How to be sure your event will make money

Now that you've come up with a great idea for a fund raiser, there's a key question you need to ask: Will the estimated profits from the event justify the time and resources your nonprofit sinks into it?

Administrator Rick Russell (Minneapolis, MN) and his board know how vitally important it is to approach special events in a businesslike way. They've designed a Special Event Prospectus that helps them decide whether or not a fund raising idea is a worthwhile idea.

The prospectus is in worksheet form, so board members can easily determine how much time, effort and resources are needed for a special event. Working through the prospectus allows the board to judge the merits of a project before any commitment is made to it.

"We don't do small fund raisers because they often don't generate enough revenue to pay for themselves," says Russell. "The prospectus stops people in their tracks as soon as they see that a project isn't going to be a moneymaker."

You'll find a copy of the prospectus at the end of this chapter (Pages 50-52). Use it to help you work through all of your ideas for special events. The results will give everyone on your board a better idea of what it takes to make an event fly! And it will clearly show you which events will actually raise money for your nonprofit.

Maximize profits from your fund raising events

To hold a successful special event, you need more than a great idea--you also need ways to pique the interest of community people. Whether you've decided on a new event, or are revitalizing one you've used before, you want to get the maximum response possible.

There are four strategies you can use to accomplish this--illustrated by the grid at the right. Take a look at the grid and decide how you can best infuse energy into all of your fund raising events.

Strategy #1: Increase the interest of previous participants in proven events.

One way to keep people coming back--and donating more money--is to enhance an "old"

Fund raising opportunities grid

	Proven event	New event
Previous participants	1	2
New participants	3	4

fund raising event with something new. Some examples...

• *Add a silent auction or raffle.* A Fort Collins, Colorado, nonprofit holds an annual "Winefest." One year, board members added a silent auction featuring seven vintage wines. Result: Profits increased $400.

A Joliet, Illinois, organization raffled off a football autographed by retired Chicago Bears star Walter Payton at its annual fund raiser. The result: An extra $800.

• *Hold a special pre-event gathering.* Administrator Gary Mrosko (Clear Lake, IA) has added an elegant pre-event dinner to his nonprofit's annual theater fund raiser. Several prominent friends of his organization invite diners to their lakefront homes before the theater showing.

"The host family entertains five or six couples over dinner and escorts them to the theater," Mrosko explains. "As a result, our profits from the event have jumped."

Strategy #2: Market a new fund raising event to previous participants.

Longtime supporters enjoy a change of pace. A brand-new event could be just the ticket to encourage them to reach deeper into their pockets.

Involve previous participants in planning the new event. When Director Joanne Martin (Burlington, ON) developed a new "Monte Carlo Night" fund raiser for her nonprofit, she phoned participants who had attended the organization's past special events and asked for their guidance.

Martin says the involvement by a large number of past participants in planning the new event helped guarantee its success. "These people not only worked as volunteers running the games, they were good paying customers in between their work shifts when they too had time to gamble," she says.

Strategy #3: Rejuvenate a standby event with new participants.

To appeal to new supporters, be more aggressive in your promotions and tune in to the special interests of potential supporters.

• *Promote your event with a multimedia campaign.* Martin says she had an eight-year-old bike-a-thon that had lost some of its punch. So she organized a media blitz.

Radio promos, TV messages, fliers sent to local schools, newspaper articles and mall displays all promoted the event to a wide audience. Plus, a volunteer dressed up as a cartoon character and handed out the fliers at local malls and stores. The result: Event participation doubled and profits tripled!

• *Ticket giveaways allow new participants to test your event at no cost.* A local radio station gave away 60 tickets to one of Martin's events and educated the public about her organization at the same time. For example, every fifth caller could win two tickets for the correct answer to a question like, "What does the organization's acronym stand for?" Giveaways also have a domino effect--the winners invite friends which means more ticket sales and profits.

● *Attract new supporters by catering to their special needs.* Administrator Kay Feurer (Springfield, IL) puts on a successful family-oriented New Year's Eve celebration. The event features shows by various entertainers within a five-block downtown area.

This year, Feurer set up a special area that was accessible to senior citizens. "We learned that many of them wanted to come but couldn't, so we took the events to them," she says.

Strategy #4: Market a new event to new participants.

This is the most risky of the four strategies, because it's striking out into unfamiliar territory. Fortunately, most new events also appeal to previous supporters, so some of that risk is reduced.

To make this strategy work, however, you need to concentrate your efforts on coming up with an event that directly appeals to your target audience. Administrator Shirley Decker (Milwaukee, WI) tells me that she wanted to attract the 18- to 35-year-old group.

So, she came up with something she thought would appeal to young adults--a frisbee throw! Participants bought chances to throw a frisbee through an open car window for a variety of prizes that included a new car. Decker made the ticket price affordable--$2 for one throw or three throws for $5. Net profit: $18,000.

Business sponsors can guarantee a profitable event

No matter what type of event you're planning, it's going to cost money to put on. Your goal is to maximize profits and minimize expenses. The simplest way to do this is to convince one or more businesses in your community to underwrite all or part of your costs for a fund raising event.

A Midwestern organization plans to raise $25,000 from its annual fund raiser. Expenses totaling $12,000, however, will cut that nearly in half, leaving the nonprofit with a net profit of only $13,000.

Business sponsorship saved the day for this nonprofit! A local grocery store has agreed to underwrite most of the fund raiser's costs. The store will also advertise the event on its grocery bags and billboards--and give free fried chicken to event-goers. Why would the grocery store go through the trouble and expense to promote the nonprofit's event? Because of the buying power of the more than 3,500 event participants, that's why!

By promoting the fund raiser, the store's name will be displayed on a banner at the event and at volunteer meetings. It will also be mentioned in each radio ad, TV public service announcement and newspaper article related to the event.

The grocery store's generosity will also receive prominent mention in the nonprofit's newsletter.

When you're looking for a business to underwrite your event, you have to do more than make an appeal to charity. You want to come up with an arrangement that <u>benefits</u> <u>both</u> <u>you</u> <u>and</u> <u>the</u> <u>business</u>.

Another important point: Businesses that underwrite fund raising events typically have similar profiles.

When you're shopping around for an event sponsor, be on the lookout for these characteristics...

● *Past event sponsorship.* A business that has sponsored an event--yours or another organization's--is a prime candidate. Keep your eyes open for businesses that underwrite fund raisers in your community--and make a list for future reference.

● *Links to your organization.* Don't overlook the obvious. Vendors who do business with your nonprofit have a self-interest in your continued success--more sales!

● *Financial ability.* Local businesses that belong to giant chains are generally high-profit operations--and often gladly return some of those profits to organizations that benefit the community.

● *The need for community visibility.* Banks are a good example of this, although other types of businesses certainly fall into the category. They see support of fund raising efforts as a way to promote themselves favorably in the community.

Corporate sponsorship can still be a great way to underwrite special event costs

Recent IRS guidelines on corporate sponsorships have raised a brouhaha with nonprofits! It started when the IRS ruled that money pumped into two college bowl football games by corporations was advertising--not a charitable donation. **The upshot is that the two nonprofits could face payment of what the IRS calls "unrelated business income tax" on corporate money they received.**

As a result, nonprofits all over the US are worried about corporate funding. But unless you're the beneficiary of extraordinarily large sponsorships, there's no need to worry, says Dick Larkin, senior manager for not-for-profit services at Price Waterhouse (Bethesda, MD). "The IRS is only looking for obvious and excessive violators of its regulations," Larkin says. "They're investigating sponsorships with millions of dollars involved, because this is where they stand to recover significant amounts in unpaid taxes."

The IRS isn't concerned with a corporate sponsor's name on Little League uniforms, ads in a special event program or a company's name on a building plaque. But Larkin offers two tips to comply with the IRS:

✓ *Make sure the corporation's name doesn't dominate your event.* For example, don't rename your special event the ABC Company Golf Classic and splash the sponsor's name all over fliers, billboards and media promotions--unless you're prepared to pay income tax on the corporation's money. Of course, it's all right to put the company's logo on your program book and tickets as long as it doesn't overshadow the event.

✓ *When you're uncomfortable with how often the company's name or logo appears,* talk it through with a corporate exec--and make sure you have your attorney or tax accountant present.

Special Event Prospectus

Date: _____ Name of event: _____

Sponsor(s) of event: _____

Description (include general description of event and purpose): _____

_____

_____

_____

Budgeted Expenses

Facility rental	$ _____
Prizes/Incentives	$ _____
Food/Refreshments	$ _____
Promotional materials	$ _____
Printing	$ _____
Postage	$ _____
Fees/Honoraria, etc	$ _____
Travel	$ _____
Other:	$ _____
Total	$ _____

Revenue Projections

Gross dollar goal $ _____

Budgeted expenses $ _____

Net dollar goal $ _____

Strategies To Generate Income

How will income be generated (pledges, at-will contributions, ticket purchases, etc)?

_____

_____

How and when will income be collected? _____

_____

_____

Incentives (raffles, door prizes) to attract participants and sponsors to the event:

_____

_____

If incentives are used, what is the plan for distribution? _____

_____

_____

Publicity/promotion to publicize event, obtain participants, etc: _____

_____

_____

General time frame: (show month and year) _____

Key volunteers recruited by: _____

_____

_____

Promotion begins: _____

Event date: _____

Organization Responsibilities

Who will be responsible for the following key activities?

Developing materials _____

Recruiting volunteers _____

Recruiting participants _____

Promotion and publicity _____

Collecting money _____

Paying expenses _____

Types (ie, committee chairperson), numbers and sources of volunteers (include methods of recruitment)

_____

_____

_____

Staff support needed:

      Staffer's Name   Responsibility   Estimated Hours

_____

_____

_____

_____

_____

Special Event Sponsor Information

Sponsor name: _____

Address: _____

Contact person: _____ Phone: _____

Type of support offered (monetary, product, space, services, etc):

_____

_____

(Photocopy sponsorship section as needed)

Given all this information, does your event idea seem feasible?   Yes   No

CHAPTER 7

How to conduct major fund raising campaigns

Lay the groundwork for your capital or
    annual campaign 54
Choose your own "best way" to ask for money 55
Spice up your campaign with special events 57
When you're faced with launching a capital
    campaign 57
When is a good time for your capital campaign? 59
Conduct a campaign feasibility study 59
A "scale of gifts" can help you reach your goal 60
Reach half your goal before going public 61
Launch your campaign in the community 62
Why should people give to your campaign? 62

Your nonprofit may decide it has to raise money to pay its general operating expenses--or it may determine that it really needs a new building or the addition of a wing. Before you consider these ambitious projects, you need to know about annual and capital campaigns.

An annual campaign is held once a year to raise money for general operating expenses. A capital campaign is a drive to raise a large sum of money over a specified time frame to pay for major new equipment or buildings. An important thing to remember about a capital campaign is that it should be a one-time appeal to meet specific, predetermined needs.

Lay the groundwork for your capital or annual campaign

Whatever type of fund raising campaign you engage in, be sure you have a thorough plan in place. If your capital or annual drive is unfocused and chaotic, the first ones to notice will be your donor prospects.

And if they're not comfortable with your campaign's image, they're sure as heck not going to contribute to it!

This is why it's imperative for your board to be as well organized as possible. Here are some tips to get you started on your campaign:

● *Set specific funding goals.* You need to know exactly how much money it will take to accomplish what you want--whether it's paying operating expenses or buying a new building. In planning your annual campaign, make sure you've considered all current and anticipated expenses. In capital campaigns, carefully look at all options for new purchases before you set a fund raising goal.

● *Pick a campaign chairperson.* Your entire board should sit down with your administrator to discuss this decision. Then you can:

1) Decide what qualifications you want your chairperson to have, such as experience, connections in the community, leadership ability and time to serve.
2) Write a job description based on what you've decided.
3) Make a list of people you know who fit this job description.
4) Select the best prospect from the list--and then ask him or her to serve.

● *Put together a solicitation packet.* Design a brochure or flyer with statistics on your nonprofit's programs and budgets. Include positive newspaper clippings about your organization in the packet--and don't leave out pledge cards for donors to complete! The packet should be eye-catching and should prominently display your nonprofit's name, address and phone number.

● *Compile or update a prospect list.* Before you mail a fund raising letter or assign board members to contact donors, be sure your prospect list is up-to-date. Once you're satisfied with the list, your board members can begin soliciting.

- *Make your first contact.* Send out your letters, make phone calls and schedule visits. Have everything you need at your fingertips when you make the initial visit.

- *Follow up your meeting.* Contact the potential donor again two weeks after the first visit. And if you can't reach the person, keep trying. Remember, persistence almost always pays off.

Choose your own "best way" to ask for money

There are many ways to approach prospects and donors as you undertake a major fund raising campaign--and each has its own advantages and drawbacks. Read through the following section, which describes the three most common approaches, and decide which is most appropriate for your nonprofit and the campaign you are about to launch.

Of course, you can mix and match any of the strategies listed, and encourage individual board members to participate in the methods that are most comfortable for them. For instance, a "rookie" fund raiser may want to start out by writing direct mail letters--and save face-to-face solicitation for the next campaign. A seasoned veteran, on the other hand, may be ready to spend all of his or her time meeting one-on-one with prospects.

- **Face-to-face**

The personal visit to a prospective donor can be an extremely effective way to build up donations to your annual or capital campaign. There is, however, one major drawback: It's easily the most time-consuming method to solicit a prospect.

If your nonprofit opts for personal visits as a way to raise funds, you might try limiting them to prospects who you know are leaning toward large donations. In any case, be sure to keep these points in mind...

1) *No face-to-face visit is a failure.* Look at all personal visits as an opportunity to educate an important segment of the public. Even if prospects say "no," they'll know more about your nonprofit than they did before you talked to them.

2) *You are not asking for yourself.* You're volunteering your time and effort for a worthwhile purpose--so don't be self-conscious about soliciting. Try to think of those who will benefit from your actions and be proud of what you're doing! Whether a prospect says "yes" or "no," you'll win his or her respect for your commitment and positive attitude.

3) *Rejection is normal.* When a prospect turns you down, take it in stride! Even with a perfect presentation and all the right touches, some people will say "no" for any number of reasons.

For instance, maybe a prospect doesn't know enough about your nonprofit to feel comfortable donating to it. If this is the case, you may have to spend some time cultivating his or her interest. Or perhaps your request for money just came at a bad time. If so, look at the situation like this: Now you know why you were turned down and you'll try again when things improve.

4) *Don't worry about not having all the answers.* Knowing all the facts about a fund raising campaign is an obvious plus, but your sincerity and enthusiasm are often even more important. Remember: A demonstrated commitment to your nonprofit's mission will go a lot further in winning a donor's trust than an ability to rattle off cold facts. So relax and just be yourself!

● **Mail**

Direct mail solicitation can bring a good return at a very low cost for your campaign. Mailings, however, have lost much of their punch in recent years. The reason probably has to do with the sheer number of organizations using this technique. This is why you need to make your mailings stand out! Try some of these tips to get your fund raising letters the attention they deserve...

1) *Make your stationery eye-catching.* "Households receive tons of fund raising letters," says Administrator Paul Easton (Youngstown, OH). "So we decided to print our solicitation letter on heart-shaped stationery. The shape of the letter was eye-catching and people took the time to read it--rather than tossing it in the wastebasket."

2) *Be selective in your mailing.* Easton and his board members sent their letter to targeted professionals capable of making potentially large donations--doctors, lawyers and engineers.

To make this approach even more effective, have board members personally mail letters to others in their own profession. For instance, if you have a doctor on your board, have him or her write and sign personalized letters to peers. Use the same techniques if your board members are contractors, teachers, ministers or executives--the options are limitless!

A word of caution: Don't solicit a potential donor by mail if the personal attention of to-do person who is accustomed to being asked face-to-face to donate may be put off by even a highly personalized letter.

● **Telemarketing**

Telemarketing is getting your nonprofit's fund raising message to potential donors over the phone. It's an effective, but difficult, technique because you must get your message across to whomever you are calling before your prospect hangs up! If you decide to use telemarketing, be sure to study these key points:

1) *The telemarketer must first establish a relationship of trust with the prospect on the other end of the line.* Be sure you identify yourself and your nonprofit so the potential donor knows you are calling about a legitimate cause.

2) *Explain the purpose of the call.* Be succinct and to the point, but sincere and friendly--it's the best way to gain the prospect's trust, especially if the person doesn't know you or your nonprofit.

3) *Don't ask questions that can be answered with a "yes" or "no" response.* Your intention is to draw the potential donor out in conversation, so you can discuss your nonprofit's needs. If the person has to answer questions in detail, you're on your way to a fruitful discussion.

4) *Once you've established trust, ask the person if he or she is interested in receiving printed material on your nonprofit's campaign.* If the person says "yes," be sure to follow up the printed materials with a phone call.

5) *Train your telemarketers to handle the variety of responses they're likely to get from donor prospects.* Teach them how to react to common objections. Why not sit down with your fellow board members and brainstorm the objections that are specific to your nonprofit's mission, philosophy and services. Be sure to spend some time working out a reply to each donor objection. Use the chart on Page 58 to write down common objections and then come up with some good replies for telemarketers to use.

Spice up your campaign with special events

In addition to these three solicitation approaches, many nonprofits will add a special event to their annual or capital campaign strategy. They may kick off their annual drive with a dinner or auction, for instance, or may make a raffle the focal point of the entire effort. Capital campaigns are often successfully launched by a highly publicized special event that's sure to bring supporters out in droves.

If you'd like to learn how a special event can be incorporated into your annual or capital campaign, turn back to Chapter 6. You'll find lots of information about a variety of events--and how you can get the greatest amount of profit from each.

When you're faced with launching a capital campaign

Sooner or later, virtually every nonprofit looks at its facilities or equipment and realizes that upgrades must be made. This is a clear signal that the time for a capital campaign has come! And sometimes this realization can be intimidating to board members.

That's because a capital campaign is a one-shot opportunity to raise money--and the amount to be raised is often very high. There are ways that you can make a capital campaign less frightening, however: Plan it well and break the overall goal into smaller, more manageable pieces.

How to respond to donor objections

Donor objection: _____

_____

_____

Our reply: _____

_____

_____

Donor objection: _____

_____

_____

Our reply: _____

_____

_____

Donor objection: _____

_____

_____

Our reply: _____

_____

_____

Donor objection: _____

_____

_____

Our reply: _____

_____

_____

When is a good time for your capital campaign?

One of the first hurdles you and your fellow board members need to get over is the temptation to wait for the "perfect" time to launch your capital campaign. Too often, boards sit around hoping their business community will report a bumper year or that the local economy will turn around.

Unfortunately, you may wait in vain, according to Administrator Roy Bynum (Perry, OK). "There's never a 'perfect time' for a capital campaign," he says. "If you wait for things in your community to improve economically, they never will. Yet your costs will continue to rise."

The key to a successful capital campaign, Bynum stresses, isn't really timing. "It's preparation--and the best way to do that is to strive daily for excellence in your nonprofit's programs and services. By meeting the community's special needs, you'll gain support for your capital campaign no matter when you launch it."

Conduct a campaign feasibility study

At some point in planning for your capital campaign, you'll want to assess your chances for success. The best method to gauge whether there is enough community support to reach your stated goal is to conduct a feasibility study.

Many boards hire a professional consultant to conduct this study for them. But with some training, you and your board peers can undertake this project yourselves. If you do so, however, remember to remain as objective as possible--you don't want to skew your results.

During a feasibility study, individuals who have the ability to make significant donations are asked if they would be willing to support your campaign. To get started, personal phone calls should be made to potential donors to set up a time for one-on-one interviews. When calling prospects, ask them if they would be willing to comment on some ideas that could have a significant impact on the future of your nonprofit.

Before the interview, it's a good idea to send a letter to the prospect explaining the purpose of your visit. Describe why you feel you must raise money for your nonprofit. Ask each potential donor to review this information before the interview.

> Key questions to ask in a feasibility study interview include:
>
> 1) Which of the needs listed are you most willing to support?
> 2) Would you participate in this campaign?
> 3) What range of contribution would you consider?
> 4) Can you list other potential donors?
> 5) What is the best way to seek community support for this campaign?
> 6) Can you suggest others who can give us their advice?

You'll find a sample copy of a feasibility study at the end of this chapter (Pages 63-66).

After major prospects have been interviewed, put the results into report form for distribution to your full board, administrator and director of development. This report will tell your nonprofit which of its needs key donors are willing to fund--and at what levels.

<u>With an indication of how successful your campaign will be, decide whether your nonprofit wants to go through with it</u>. This is where board teamwork really comes into play! Be sure that all board members participate in the discussion of the study.

If the feasibility study clearly shows you don't have enough of a donor base to get your capital campaign off the ground, you need to take time to analyze the study's findings. This information will give you the best clues to why the community support isn't there for your campaign.

There could be several explanations for this lack of enthusiasm about your campaign. For instance, potential donors may not be as aware of your nonprofit as you would like them to be. If this is the case, you'll need to concentrate your efforts on public relations to make your nonprofit and the services it provides better known.

Maybe you'll need to modify your campaign plans slightly to better fit the needs of the community--or you may have set your goal unrealistically high. So take a hard look at what the results are telling you.

A "scale of gifts" can help you reach your goal

After some careful scrutiny, your board decides to launch your capital campaign. But where do you start?!

One of the most effective tools you can use to help convince donors to dig deeply into their pockets is called a "<u>Scale</u> <u>of</u> <u>Gifts</u>." As you can see by the chart on the right, a scale of gifts lets you see at a glance how many--and what size--gifts you need.

This chart not only helps you stay on course as you're soliciting contributions, it can also be a powerful motivator for prospects. For example, a person who has seen your chart might say, "I see you need one gift of $50,000 to meet your campaign goal. I'll give you that $50,000!"

Before you begin approaching donors during your capital campaign, have your board draw up its own scale of gifts chart, depending on the total

Scale of gifts chart for a $225,000 campaign

Number of gifts	Gift size
1	$ 50,000
2	$ 20,000
4	$ 10,000
6	$ 5,000
9	$ 2,500
10	$ 1,000
15	$ 500
24	$ 250
50	$ 100
100	$ 50
200	$ 25
200	$ 20
TOTAL	$225,000

amount you'd like to raise. As you put the chart together, keep the following points in mind:

> 1) Remember the 80/20 rule--in any capital campaign, it's a safe bet to assume that 80% of your goal will be contributed by 20% of your donors.
> 2) Organize giving levels to reflect the size and number of gifts you've received from donors in the past.
> 3) Remember that the number of gifts goes up as their dollar amount decreases.

When you start soliciting, a good rule to follow is to go after gifts on the top of your chart. First ask donor prospects interviewed during your feasibility study. These people have been involved in the planning stages of your campaign, and they'll expect you to return and ask for their pledges. Then go after the medium-sized and smaller gifts in that order.

Reach half your goal before going public

One of the most important rules that govern capital campaigns is to hold off announcing your campaign to the public until you've reached half your fund raising goal.

Administrator Rick Peterson (Stroudsburg, PA) tells me that there's a key psychological reason for waiting until then. Here's how he explains it:

"Before you start soliciting donations from the general public, you have to convince them that your campaign is a success," he says. "If you don't have a good amount of money in hand before you go public, it will be hard to get donations out of people.

"People might think your campaign is going to fail--or that you'll quit before you reach the goal and the money won't be used for its intended purpose."

According to Peterson, the best place to get started raising half your goal is with your own board. Major board member donations at his nonprofit helped get a $600,000 fund raising campaign off the ground. Here's how Peterson was able to persuade them to give...

"They were involved in the planning from the start. I just said, 'OK, it's time to put our money where our mouth is. It's going to be hard to ask others to give if we who know our organization best haven't.' The board came through with $50,000."

After you've gotten initial board member support, quietly go to other donors to help you reach that all important half-way mark. Try asking donors capable of giving large amounts for "leadership commitment" gifts!

Tell these people how important they are to your nonprofit, let them know you thought of them first and then show your appreciation for their help in getting your campaign off to a good start.

Another effective way to approach major donors at the beginning of a campaign is to go after "<u>challenge gifts</u>." Ask for a large contribution from a prospect, but on the condition that it be given to your nonprofit only when your board raises a specific amount first.

The beauty of this method is that it inspires board members to put forth that extra effort, a Michigan administrator tells me. "Our nonprofit solicited a challenge gift for $5,000, with the donor's stipulation that we had to raise an equal amount first," she says. "When my board members realized that every dollar of what they raised was actually two dollars--doubling the challenge--they really went to work!"

Launch your campaign in the community

Now that you've reached that key 50% of your campaign goal, you're ready to start asking for general contributions, using the approaches outlined earlier in this chapter.

Before you go public, be sure you can explain to people why they should contribute to your campaign. Think about the services that your nonprofit provides. Can you show the public how reaching your funding goal will benefit the community?

Why should people give money to your campaign?
1)
2)
3)
4)
5)

Feasibility Study

Person interviewed: _____

Occupation: _____

Address: _____

Business telephone: _____ Home telephone: _____

Business and community organizations

Civic: _____

Donor: _____

Board Member: _____

Professional Associations: _____

Other: _____

_____

(Information above this line provided by preliminary research.)

1. What is your general opinion of our nonprofit?

    ❏ Excellent ❏ Good ❏ Fair ❏ Poor

    Reason: _____

    _____

    _____

    _____

    _____

2. To your knowledge, what is the public opinion or image of our organization?

    Reason: _____

    _____

    _____

    _____

(more)

Feasibility Study (continued)

(Interviewer--Before you ask the following questions, be sure you have explained what your nonprofit has planned in terms of your capital campaign. It's important that the person you interview understands your purpose.)

3. Based on the facts as you now understand them, do you feel a financial program is needed to raise the funds necessary to provide proposed services and programs?

    ❏ Yes   ❏ No

    Reason: _____

    _____

    _____

    _____

    Suggestions: _____

    _____

    _____

    _____

4. Do general economic conditions and public attitudes favor a campaign in the near future for capital gifts?

    ❏ Yes   ❏ No

5. Will the community support a $ _____ (fill in dollar goal) fund raising program?

    ❏ Yes   ❏ No

    If no, what amount do you feel could be raised? $ _____

6. Is it possible to obtain one gift of 10% to 20% of the total goal?

    ❏ Yes   ❏ No

    If yes, from whom could we expect this type of gift? _____

    _____

(more)

Feasibility Study (continued)

7. List 10 individuals, businesses or foundations that could donate a major portion of the goal:

   1. _____
   2. _____
   3. _____
   4. _____
   5. _____
   6. _____
   7. _____
   8. _____
   9. _____
   10. _____

8. Would a gift of $2,500, $5,000 or $10,000 be possible from any of the individuals, businesses or foundations named above? (Please indicate an amount next to the name.)

9. Would you be willing to give your time to a committee or assist in some other capacity?

   ❏ Yes   ❏ No

   If yes, in what capacity? _____
   _____

10. Would you consider supporting this campaign financially?

    ❏ Yes   ❏ No

    If yes, how much would you consider? _____

11. Would your corporation (or your employer) make a substantial gift on a three- to five-year basis?

    ❏ Yes   ❏ No

    If yes, how much would the gift be? _____

(more)

Feasibility Study (continued)

12. What do you consider the best way to seek community support for this campaign?

_____

_____

_____

_____

13. Please suggest five community leaders who might serve as campaign chairs:

1. _____

2. _____

3. _____

4. _____

5. _____

14. Can you suggest any other community leaders whose experience and opinions we should solicit regarding this campaign?

_____

_____

_____

15. Are there any points not covered in this interview that you would like to discuss?

_____

_____

_____

16. General comments and/or suggestions?

_____

_____

_____

CHAPTER 8

Planned giving is an excellent source of money for your nonprofit

Planned giving offers your donors more flexibility.......68
Board contributions give endowment fund initial
 boost..69
Check out other organizations' endowment funds...... 70
Vary your planned giving options.................................. 70
Life insurance agents can be a big help to your
 nonprofit...74
Your local banker holds the key to trusts
 and foundations... 74

Another important fund raising source for your nonprofit--one that is often misunderstood--is <u>planned giving</u>. It's downright disturbing how much confusion surrounds those two words nowadays. I've lost count of the times I've heard about "how complicated" planned giving is.

<u>Planned giving is simply a gift that a donor arranges well ahead of time, most commonly through life insurance, wills, memorials and other ways</u>. I suggest that you read this chapter carefully to learn how your nonprofit can benefit from the different methods of planned giving.

Before you start, think about your nonprofit's needs--like new construction or program expansion--that could be met through a planned giving program. Now write them down:

1) _____

2) _____

3) _____

4) _____

5) _____

Keep this list in front of you as a "motivator" for those moments when you find yourself despairing of even getting your planned giving program off the ground!

Planned giving offers your donors more flexibility

One of the main advantages of planned giving is that it often results in sizeable donations to your nonprofit. This flows naturally from one of its built-in features: It allows donors who can't produce large cash gifts now to give handsomely down the road.

For example, very few donors have $100,000 in a checking account just waiting for your nonprofit. Many of these donors, however, own assets that can be of great benefit to you. Just think for a minute about the people on your prospect list. How many of them own businesses or real estate? How many own extensive stocks, bonds or securities?

While these donors can't give a large cash gift, they might consider setting up a trust fund for your nonprofit or including it in their wills. Other common planned gifts include life insurance policies and bequests of property or equipment. Consider these tips to help your board raise funds through planned giving...

● *Learn all you can about planned giving.* Some administrators I know tell me their boards are often reluctant to undertake a planned giving program--they think it's too technical. The solution to this problem is to have your board meet with financial planners, attorneys or bankers to learn how planned giving works. "Once you have good information and know what you're doing, a planned giving program doesn't seem so overwhelming," one New York administrator tells me.

● *Take your time.* A planned giving program doesn't happen overnight. "You need to build donor support," says Administrator Suzanne Behr (Omaha, NE), whose board spent three years working on its program. "You need to make sure you have community recognition before you undertake something like this." Behr's board held high-profile special events and an annual campaign before beginning a planned giving program.

● *Publicize your program!* Unless prospective donors know about your planned giving program, you'll receive precious few donations! Here's how Behr's board members aggressively solicit planned giving...

1) By making visits to regular donors to discuss their planned giving program.
2) By distributing information about their program to estate-planning professionals like lawyers, bankers and financial planners, who are then asked to mention the nonprofit to clients.
3) By sending brochures explaining the program to people on their mailing list.

Board contributions give endowment fund initial boost

Once you've decided to go ahead with a planned giving program, you need to consider how you'll manage the gifts you receive. The most common way to do this is through an endowment.

In a fund of this kind, gifts are typically invested in stocks, certificates of deposit or government bonds--with income from the investment going to meet the needs of a nonprofit.

Because laws affecting endowment funds vary by state, I strongly recommend that you talk to an attorney before you start one.

Let's say that you've started an endowment fund. What's your next step? Obviously, you'd like to see it grow--but where do you begin? Administrator Robert Hutson (Washington, DC) says his board believes so strongly in its nonprofit's mission that board members began their endowment fund by contributing a million dollars themselves! Sound like the impossible dream come true? Actually, it was accomplished with shocking simplicity. Here's how...

Ten board members donated the money needed to pay the premiums on ten $100,000 life insurance policies--with the recipient organization (their nonprofit) named as beneficiary!

According to Hutson, leading by example is a powerful marketing tool for a nonprofit's board in its planned giving program. "If you can go to others and point out that your board members are so strongly committed that they've established a solid financial foundation for your organization--it's bound to have an impact," he tells me.

Check out other organizations' endowment funds

When you're starting an endowment, it's always wise to get expert advice. Colleges, hospitals and larger nonprofits frequently have endowment funds. Make a list of organizations that are likely to have endowments, along with their development directors or administrators. Now begin calling names on the list to make appointments to discuss the feasibility of your own endowment fund.

Organization	Development Director or Administrator	Phone

Vary your planned giving options

Before researching planned giving and endowments, you probably had little or no idea how they worked. The same thing can be said about most of the people you solicit for planned giving programs. As a board member, it rests on you to explain the options to them--and the ways each one is mutually beneficial for your nonprofit and the donor.

If you're asking a donor to include your nonprofit in his or her will, remind the person that a planned gift is really a deferred donation. It doesn't require an immediate gift, but it does guarantee that a contribution will be made in the future.

Consider these options when you discuss planned giving with prospective donors...

1) Memorial gifts

Many times a donor will want to leave a gift to your nonprofit in memory of a deceased family member or friend. This type of gift--a memorial gift--will be a special gift for the giver because it will always be a reminder of the loved one whom it was given for.

Development Director Bryan Zindren's organization (Terre Haute, IN) uses two strategies to maintain his nonprofit's successful memorial giving program. Here's what he does...

● His organization's business reply envelope has a memorial giving form on the back. The form accompanies all mailings, giving donors a continual opportunity to make memorial gifts.

● Service groups are asked to present information on Zindren's memorial giving program at meetings--and to distribute memorial cards to their members. "There are 120 Knights of Columbus councils in our state and a large percent of our memorial givers are KCs," he says. "Service clubs are an excellent source of memorial gifts because they always honor their deceased members."

Remember: A memorial gift is in memory of a deceased person. If you want a successful program, be sure you are sensitive to the needs of families being asked to give. Most families who give a memorial gift may still be hurting from the loss of the deceased person.

> Here are points to observe when accepting memorial gifts:
>
> * Let the family members know you have received their gift in honor of a loved one.
> * Send a sympathy card and let the family know you share in their sorrow.
> * Appropriately recognize the memorial gift in your newsletters or mailing.

2) Gifts from wills and bequests

Asking a donor to include your nonprofit in his or her will is often an excellent way to bring in a large sum of money. The catch, however, is that many donors are reluctant to think about their own death--let alone about giving away money or property.

So you'll probably need to spend some time explaining why making out a will is so important. Let the potential donor know what can happen to his or her estate if there is no will. For example, not leaving a will can result in a court battle--with costly legal fees--among surviving relatives.

Although it's only natural to think that wealthy people would be the ones to target for asking to be included in a will, don't overlook the not-so-wealthy people.

"The trend I see is more gifts through wills from people with middle-level incomes," says Administrator Gary Mrosko (Clear Lake, IA). "The majority of our donors have modest incomes.

"That's why we want all donors to identify with the idea of naming our organization as beneficiary in their wills. We've received bequests from donors' wills which range from $500 to $150,000."

Even small bequests can add up, adds Mrosko. A year ago, for instance, his nonprofit collected $96,000 in bequests--30% of which were less than $10,000.

"People who regularly donate small amounts are often overlooked because they're not the stereotypic wealthy most nonprofits target for gifts through wills," he says.

"But they're often tickled pink when you show appreciation for their modest gifts--and they may have much more to give than you know about.

"For example, one individual gave us $200 and we sent a personal thank-you. He was so impressed by our consideration, that he responded by donating $15,000 in a planned gift."

The key in seeking gifts through wills is to realize that donors don't have to leave everything they own to your nonprofit, stresses Mrosko.

"They can distribute their estate among family--and still help your nonprofit by naming it as beneficiary of only 1% to 5% of their estate.

"Once you realize the significance a small bequest can have on your nonprofit's budget--and that it's not going to hurt the donor's financial situation--it's easier to talk to friends and acquaintances about gifts through bequests."

3) Gifts through life insurance policies

Gifts of life insurance are an invaluable source of money for a nonprofit's planned giving program. With a minimum amount of cash, a well-intentioned donor can make a contribution that's worth tens of thousands of dollars!

Here's how charitable gifts of life insurance can work for your nonprofit:

Let's say a 35-year-old donor buys a $25,000 whole life insurance policy. This person then names your nonprofit as both owner and beneficiary of the policy.

The donor makes annual gifts to your organization equal to the premium payments on the life insurance policy--about $500 a year. The gift is tax-deductible because it's made to a nonprofit organization. Your organization then makes the premium payments to the insurance company.

<u>When the donor dies, your organization receives the insurance policy's benefits--a nice amount of money in return for the minor administrative task of paying the premium on the policy</u>!

(Note: Donors can also transfer existing insurance policies to your organization by simply signing a few papers.)

A great way to let the public know about donating life insurance policies to your nonprofit is to <u>team up with a local insurance agent</u>. You'll find that agents are enthusiastic promoters of charitable gifts of life insurance policies.

The reason is simple enough to explain: Insurance reps want to sell more policies. Many see the promotion of charitable giving through life insurance as an excellent sales opportunity.

Insurance Agent Keith Fogt (Houston, TX) sells customers on the idea of donating the full value of their life insurance policies to charities. And it's been a real boon for his insurance business.

"It gives me an opportunity to show people how they can have a big impact on the charity of their choice through life insurance," he explains.

"Instead of just giving $100 outright to a charity, they can use that money to pay premiums on a life insurance policy. Then they know the charity will receive a large amount later. Although $100 doesn't seem like very much, a $10,000 policy is a significant contribution," adds Fogt. "And they still get a tax deduction for the gift."

This approach has been mutually beneficial for Fogt and two local organizations. In one year, he's sold 138 policies designated to two nonprofits. The value of the policies: $1.25 million!

Advantages of life insurance gifts for the donor:	Advantages of life insurance gifts for your nonprofit:
* The donor has the potential to give a gift much larger than the actual premiums paid. * The life insurance policy doesn't affect the donor's will or estate plan since it's owned by the recipient organization. * Donor contributions are tax-deductible.	* It's an exceptional opportunity to receive major gifts. * Life insurance policies provide substantial cash values which your organization may borrow from. * Because your organization is both owner and beneficiary of the policy, the gift is irrevocable. In other words, the donor can't change his or her mind once the gift has been made.

Life insurance agents can be a big help to your nonprofit

Take a couple of minutes and jot down some of the insurance agents you know who would be interested in working with your nonprofit. Remember to let them know working together will benefit both of you!

Agent	Company	Best board member to contact the agent

Your local banker holds the key to trusts and foundations

Once your planned giving program is up and running, there's an important fund raising resource right in your community: your local bank trust officer who oversees family trusts and foundations.

"It's the bank trust officer's job to find appropriate programs and to disburse the money," says Development Director Lisa Porter (Kansas City, KS). Her organization receives money from five family trusts or foundations, with amounts ranging from $2,000 to $50,000.

In a family trust, a person has established a special account to distribute his or her financial resources to family members and charities. The trust account is usually administered by the trust officer of a bank.

A family foundation is set up strictly to oversee a person's charitable contributions. Again, a bank trust officer often administers the funds.

The key to getting the funds is personal contacts with bank trust officers, says Porter. This is where board members can capitalize on their personal contacts.

"I go to a banker, tell him about my programs and that I'm looking for funds," she explains. "The banker may sit on six or seven trust boards. If my program doesn't fit the specific purpose of a family foundation or trust he or she administers, the information can be passed along to board members of other trusts.

"The banker serves as a contact person for the trust or foundation. He sets up an interview between the family and myself," Porter says. "From there, it's up to me to sell my program. The family usually wants an in-depth look at our services. So I set up a facility tour and meetings with a program director or client. I also share case studies of clients who've been helped by our services.

"Trusts are usually good about renewing funds every year," she adds. "They may go for small increments over a long period--say $2,000 to $3,000 a year. Or a trust may give you $50,000 over a three-year period. Family foundations are also good about supporting ongoing programs."

Get acquainted with your local bank trust officers, advises Porter. "Explain your programs and need for funds. You can't ask for names of family trusts because those are confidential. But you can use the banker as the liaison."

Printed in Dunstable, United Kingdom